SPOTLIGHT ON CIVIC ACTION

MAJORITY RULE VS. INDIVIDUAL RIGHTS

ERIKA MEERSMAN

PowerKiDS press™

NEW YORK

Published in 2018 by The Rosen Publishing Group, Inc.
29 East 21st Street, New York, NY 10010

Editor: Elizabeth Krajnik
Book Design: Michael Flynn
Interior Layout: Rachel Rising

Photo Credits: Cover Caiaimage/Robert Daly/OJO+/Getty Images; p. 5 Anadolu Agency/Anadolu Agency/Getty Images; pp. 7, 29 Rawpixel.com/Shutterstock.com; pp. 9, 13 (background) Evgeny Karandaev/Shutterstock.com; pp. 9, 13 (documents) Courtesy of the U.S. National Archives and Records Administration; p. 11 vipflash/Shutterstock.com; p. 15 https://en.wikipedia.org/wiki/File:The_Gerry-Mander_Edit.png; p. 16 Mireya Acierto/DigitalVision/Getty Images; p. 17 careylj/Shutterstock.com; p. 19 Christopher Penler/Shutterstock.com; p. 20 PointImages/Shutterstock.com; p. 21 D.Somsup/Shutterstock.com; p. 23 bakdc/Shutterstock.com; p. 24 Apic/Hulton Archive/Getty Images; p. 25 Bettmann/Bettmann/Getty Images; p. 27 Gilbert Carrasquillo/Getty Images Entertainment/Getty Images.

Cataloging-in-Publication Data

Names: Meersman, Erika.
Title: Majority rule vs. individual rights / Erika Meersman.
Description: New York : PowerKids Press, 2018. | Series: Spotlight on civic action | Includes index.
Identifiers: ISBN 9781538327920 (pbk.) | ISBN 9781508163947 (library bound) | ISBN 9781538328040 (6 pack)
Subjects: LCSH: Representative government and representation--Juvenile literature. | Civil rights--Juvenile literature. | Human rights--Juvenile literature.
Classification: LCC JC571.M44 2018 | DDC 323--dc23

Manufactured in China

CPSIA Compliance Information: Batch #BW18PK For further information contact Rosen Publishing, New York, New York at 1-800-237-9932.

CONTENTS

CHAPTER ONE

WHAT'S A MAJORITY?

Majorities can be found everywhere. How many girls are in your class? How many boys are in your class? The group that has more than half the members is the majority. At any given time, the U.S. Congress has a majority party, which is the one more American citizens voted for. In 2017, the Republican Party was the majority party in both the Senate and the House of Representatives. This means that all other political parties had a minority of representatives at that time. President Donald Trump is also a Republican.

The U.S. government relies on majorities for many situations. A majority vote is required to pass a bill from one chamber of Congress to the next. In the House, a majority is 218 of 435 votes. In the Senate, a majority is 51 of 100 votes.

President Donald Trump won the 2016 presidential election because a majority of electors in the **Electoral College** voted for him.

CHAPTER TWO

MAJORITY RULE

Majority rule refers to the control a majority has in decision-making situations. When two groups can't agree on something, they may vote to settle the disagreement. The winning group must win by over 50 percent. When a majority wins a decision by just a few votes, it may seem unfair to the side that didn't win. If a minority prevents a majority from making a decision, this could turn into minority rule. A well-known example of minority rule applies to the white minority ruling South Africa during **apartheid**.

Some people mix up majority rule with a plurality system. A plurality system means that a person running for office wins by receiving more votes than all the other candidates. This system is different from a majority system because the winning candidate doesn't need to win more votes than all other candidates combined. Electing U.S. officials for public office is most commonly done by plurality.

Majority rule is simple: Only one side wins and it's clear which side that is. The group with the larger number of people is likely to win.

CHAPTER THREE

MAJORITY RULE IN THE UNITED STATES

Some form of majority rule has existed in the United States since the country declared itself independent of Great Britain in 1776. The Founding Fathers made sure that the American people would be able to govern themselves. Majority rule allows the people's popular will, or desire, to become **policy**. The U.S. Constitution was written to protect the rights of American citizens from politicians or majorities who might try to take advantage of their positions of power. The U.S. Congress was created both to represent the American people and to make sure that majority rule doesn't become **tyrannical**.

In the United States, there are several different ways majorities rule. In Congress, majorities of different sizes are required to make certain decisions. For example, to propose an **amendment** to the U.S. Constitution, both chambers of Congress must agree with a two-thirds majority, which means two-thirds of the representatives present must vote in favor of the amendment.

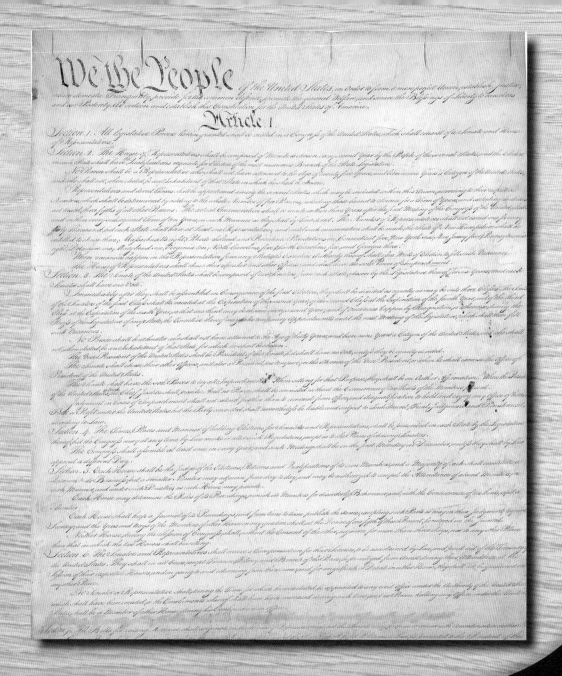

Amendments to the U.S. Constitution protect U.S. citizens from political **abuses** of power. The Constitution originally stated that state legislators would choose members of the Senate. It was amended to allow people to vote for their senators directly.

Even though majority rule is often a quick and easy way to make a decision, it isn't always the fairest way to do so. Quite often in U.S. politics, majority rule can lead to the members of the majority party concerning themselves only with issues they want to solve rather than listening to everyone's needs and suggestions.

One way to prevent people's opinions from being ignored in government is to require a supermajority for certain decisions. A supermajority is a majority greater than a simple majority of more than half a group. For example, a supermajority could be 60 percent, two-thirds, or three-fourths of the group. Supermajorities are only required in very special cases, such as proposing amendments to the U.S. Constitution. Supermajorities are meant to prevent "tyranny of the majority," which can lead to the rights of the minority party or parties being ignored.

A supermajority of two-thirds in both the House and the Senate can override the president's choice to **veto** a bill. On September 28, 2016, the House and the Senate overrode President Barack Obama's veto of a bill allowing families of the victims of the September 11, 2001, terrorist attacks to sue the Saudi Arabian government.

CHAPTER FOUR

TOO POWERFUL

Sometimes majority rule can **oppress** minority opinion. The Founding Fathers tried to prevent this by creating the three branches of government and a system of checks and balances. However, the opinions of a political minority can often go unheard and the larger majority group may abuse their rights.

Checks and balances help make sure that government decisions are fair. By having bills go through different checkpoints, people's individual rights are protected. Because of this ability to check each other, no one branch of government can become too powerful.

Some leaders elected to a position of power by a majority of citizens, such as Adolf Hitler in Germany, seized complete control. These people are called dictators. As long as the citizens of democratic countries fight for the liberties of all citizens, dictators won't rise to power.

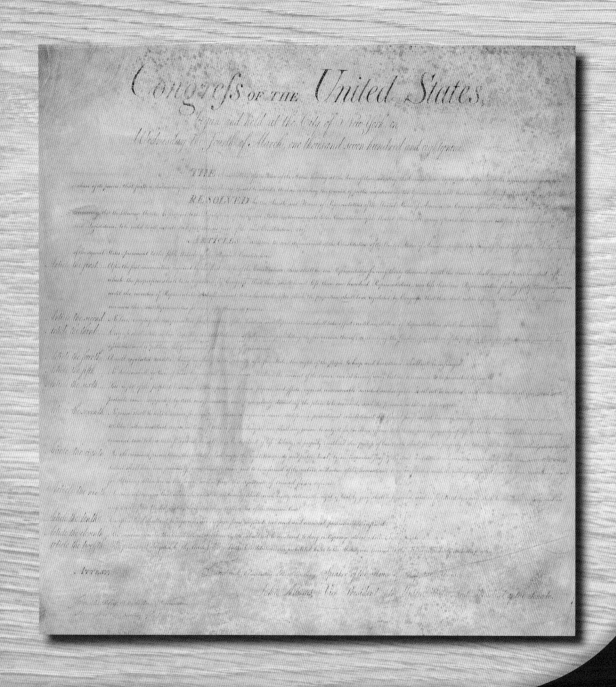

Each U.S. citizen has individual rights. These rights are outlined in the Bill of Rights.

CHAPTER FIVE

GERRYMANDERING

Gerrymandering is the process of redrawing voting districts in order to throw off election results in favor of one political party. Ideally, an elected candidate should reflect the population living in a given area. Often, the party that controls the state government gets to choose how district lines are drawn. This can result in gerrymandering

This process is very common in America, and yet most voting Americans agree that the process should be done away with. Gerrymandering often favors the majority party in the state and federal governments. This can be a large issue in terms of individual rights because it makes citizens feel powerless. This feeling often results in decreased voter turnout. As a consequence, the candidate who best represents those voters is less likely to win the election.

The labels within the illustration read: METHUEN, HAVERHILL, AMESBURY, SALSBURY, BRADFORD, N. PORT, NEWBURY, ANDOVER, ROXFORD, ROWLEY, MIDDLETON, TOPSFIELD, IPSWICH, LYNNFIELD, DANVERS, WENHAM, HAMILTON, BEVERLY, MANCHESTER, CLOCESTER, SALEM, LYNN, MARBLE HEAD, CHELSEA

The term "gerrymander" comes from this political cartoon from 1812, which depicts the redrawing of electoral districts in Massachusetts. Massachusetts governor Elbridge Gerry approved rearranging district lines—creating a district shaped somewhat like a salamander—for political gain.

CHAPTER SIX

WHAT ARE INDIVIDUAL RIGHTS?

The main part of the U.S. Constitution doesn't say much about the individual rights of U.S. citizens. In 1791, the Bill of Rights, which is the first 10 amendments to the U.S. Constitution, was **ratified**. It outlines many of the individual rights of citizens. The First Amendment gives U.S. citizens the freedom to practice whichever religion they choose and establishes freedom of speech and the press. It also prevents Congress from passing laws that keep people from exercising these rights.

U.S. citizens' right to practice any religion—or none at all—is protected by the First Amendment. Muslims only make up about 1 percent of the U.S. population, but their religious rights are as important as those of the people who practice more common religions, such as Christianity.

However, these rights aren't the only rights U.S. citizens have. Congress has passed other amendments to the U.S. Constitution. The 13th Amendment abolished, or got rid of, slavery. This protects people's individual right to not be forced to work against their will.

Some of these amendments might not apply to all American citizens directly, but all of them influence how the U.S. government handles certain situations. The government has the power to limit our actions with laws, which can affect our individual rights.

CHAPTER SEVEN

PROTECTING YOUR INDIVIDUAL RIGHTS

Some people's rights are abused by government policy. For example, some U.S. laws once made it legal to **discriminate** against African Americans. In the 1960s, people fought for equal rights for all U.S. citizens and an end to racial **segregation**. Because of their hard work, Congress passed the Civil Rights Act of 1964, which makes discrimination based on race, color, religion, sex, and national origin illegal.

How can you protect your individual rights? First, you should educate yourself about your rights. Then you can determine if someone's actions toward you are illegal. Many people have taken their cases to court. Sometimes a group called the American Civil Liberties Union (ACLU) becomes involved.

The First Amendment of the U.S. Constitution gives American citizens the freedom to assemble peacefully, the freedom of association, and the freedom of speech. Americans have the right to protest their government when they are unhappy with government policies.

American citizens are responsible for making sure they protect their rights. For example, the Fifth Amendment says that American citizens have the right to protect their private property from public use. Sometimes local governments want to use people's land to build roads or public buildings. To do this, the government must purchase the land from the landowner. If the landowner doesn't understand and protect their rights, they risk losing them.

If there are problems in your school, school board meetings are a great place to bring these problems to light. During most meetings, there's is a time when the public can speak.

One of the best ways to protect your rights is to become educated about what your rights are and work toward protecting them for all Americans. Taking action can be scary and difficult, but bringing your concerns to officials at the lowest levels of the local government is a great place to start.

CHAPTER EIGHT

THE JUDICIAL SYSTEM

The U.S. judicial system, or the system of courts in the United States, also works to protect individual rights. The U.S. Supreme Court and lower federal courts protect citizens' individual rights by interpreting the Constitution and its amendments. Each state makes and interprets its own laws. State courts most often interpret state law.

In the United States, there are several different types of courts. At the state level, there are circuit courts, **appellate** courts, and a supreme court. At the federal level, there are district courts, appellate courts, and the U.S. Supreme Court. Each type of court deals with certain types of issues. Because the Constitution limits the federal government's power, the federal court system only hears certain kinds of cases. Most court cases are heard in state courts.

The U.S. Supreme Court only hears cases that involve federal law or government or involve disagreements between two parties who aren't from the same state or country. The Scopes trial (see pages 24 and 25) and the *Roe v. Wade* case (see pages 26 and 27) dealt with state laws that some people felt were unconstitutional.

CHAPTER NINE

THE SCOPES TRIAL OF 1925

In 1859, English scientist Charles Darwin published *On the Origin of Species*. This book discusses how animals and plants have the ability to develop into new species over very long periods of time. This process is known as evolution. The theory of evolution became a very **controversial** topic among some religious groups.

JOHN T. SCOPES

SCOPES TRIAL

In 1968, the Supreme Court ruled in *Epperson v. State of Arkansas* that preventing public schools from teaching evolution is unconstitutional because it promotes one religion for all people. Individuals in the United States are free to choose their own religion or none at all.

One of the first issues the ACLU tackled was the ban on teaching the theory of evolution in Tennessee schools. After the state passed the ban (called the Butler Act) in March 1925, the ACLU had biology teacher John T. Scopes teach it in his classes anyway. Scopes was sued and the ACLU and lawyer Clarence Darrow defended him in court. Scopes was found guilty but the Butler Act wasn't enforced again. Similar laws were defeated in other states over the next several years.

CHAPTER TEN

ROE V. WADE

Abortion, or the medical procedure that ends a pregnancy, is one of the most controversial issues the ACLU has tackled. In 1970, Norma L. McCorvey (Jane Roe) and her lawyers filed a court case against Henry Wade, the Dallas County district attorney. Roe's case claimed a Texas law that banned most abortions in the state was unconstitutional. A Texas federal court ruled the law was unconstitutional, but Wade requested that the ruling be looked at by a higher court. In 1973, the U.S. Supreme Court agreed that the Texas law was unconstitutional.

According to the ruling, choosing to have an abortion falls under an individual's "zone of privacy." This means that receiving an abortion is a private thing, and states don't have the right to control this activity. *Roe v. Wade* is one of the Supreme Court's most famous rulings and continues to be controversial today.

Abortion has long been a divisive topic in U.S. society. Many Americans fight to keep abortion legal. Many other Americans fight against it.

CHAPTER ELEVEN

AMERICA: A MAJORITY MINORITY

A majority minority occurs when a minority group, or group of minority groups, becomes the majority population in a state or district in the United States. In 2014, the U.S. Census Bureau reported that there were more than 20 million children under 5 years old living in the United States. Of these children, 50.2 percent belonged to minority groups. The largest single minority group—22 percent of the 20 million children—was composed of white children from Hispanic backgrounds. African American children represented 15 percent of the 20 million. These numbers are expected to rise.

As the percentage of minorities in the U.S. population continues to increase, legislation and representation in the government will likely change. Candidates for political office may have to work harder to gain the support of members of the majority minority. This means that minority groups will have a greater chance of having their needs met in the government.

In recent years, American schools have enrolled more students from minority groups than white students.

CHAPTER TWELVE

WHAT'S YOUR EXPERIENCE?

Have you ever been part of a majority group? Have you ever been a part of a minority group? What challenges did you face and how did you overcome them?

When thinking about the U.S. government, considering these questions is very important. Majority representation in the government allows representatives to make decisions on behalf of the larger part of the population. However, when minority groups win representation in public offices, it allows other people's opinions to be heard and considered in important legislation.

People have several options to have their voices heard. Individuals of all walks of life can participate in protests, which allow their voices to be heard by large groups of people. Supporting your fellow Americans is a great way to make sure that U.S. citizens' rights are being upheld in the government.

GLOSSARY

abuse (uh-BYOOS) Wrong or unfair treatment or use.

amendment (uh-MEHND-muhnt) A change in the words or meaning of a law or document, such as a constitution.

apartheid (uh-PAR-tyt) A former policy of segregation and political and economic discrimination against non-European groups in the Republic of South Africa.

appellate (uh-PEH-luht) Of or relating to appeals, or the legal action by which a court case is brought to a higher court for review, or the power to hear appeals.

controversial (kahn-truh-VUHR-shuhl) Likely to give rise to disagreement.

discriminate (dis-KRIH-muh-nayt) To treat people unequally based on class, race, or religion.

Electoral College (ih-LEK-tuh-ruhl KAH-lihj) A body of 538 elected representatives who cast votes to elect the president and vice president.

oppress (uh-PRES) To control or rule in a harsh or cruel way.

policy (PAH-luh-see) A set of guidelines or rules that determine a course of action.

ratify (RAA-tuh-fy) To formally approve.

segregation (seh-grih-GAY-shuhn) The separation of people based on race, class, or ethnicity.

tyrannical (tuh-RAA-nih-kuhl) Having to do with the use of power over people in a way that is cruel and unfair.

veto (VEE-toh) To prevent from becoming law.

INDEX

PRIMARY SOURCE LIST

Page 9
Constitution of the United States. Created by the Constitutional Convention. 1787. Now kept at the National Archives, Washington, D.C.

Page 13
Bill of Rights. 1789. Now kept at the National Archives, Washington, D.C.

Page 15
"The Gerry-Mander." Cartoon. Published in the *Boston Gazette* on March 26, 1812. Now kept at the Library of Congress Newspaper, Serials and Government Publications Division, Washington, D.C.

WEBSITES

Due to the changing nature of Internet links, PowerKids Press has developed an online list of websites related to the subject of this book. This site is updated regularly. Please use this link to access the list: www.powerkidslinks.com/sociv/majrule